MINING NATURES TREASURES WITH JIM AND DAVE

BATTERIES, BONFIRES AND BEACH TOWELS

By

JIM MELLOS

Copyright © 2017

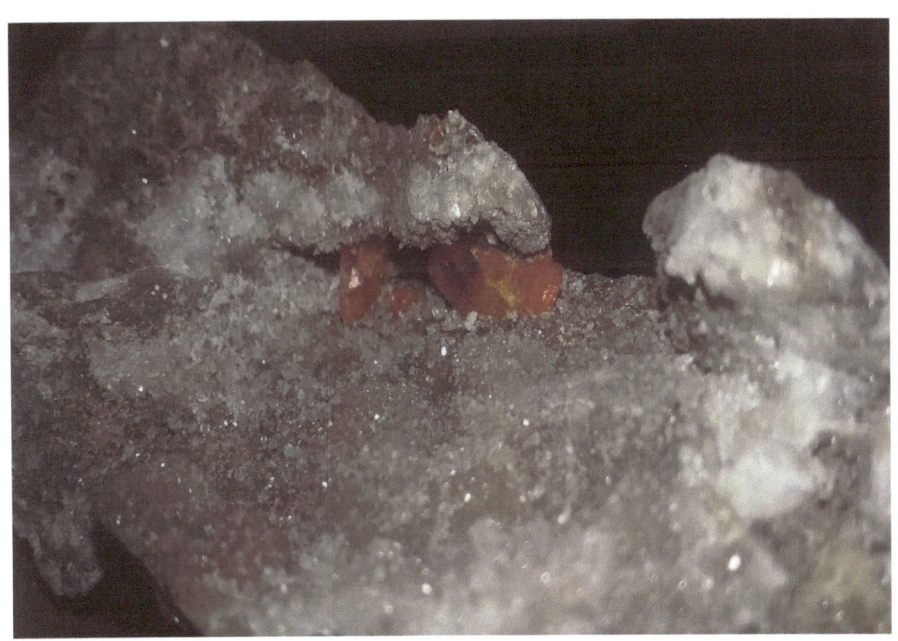

INTRODUCTION

Wulfenite. The mineral that is formed by super-heated mineral rich water being forced up from deep within the earth and into the cracks in the bedrock. The minerals collect on each other as the water slowly cools and recedes leaving the cracks and pockets lined with fluorite and wulfenite crystals.

This is what Dave and I were searching for. The red orange crystals were calling to us and we just had to respond. Would this be the day we strike it rich or will we strike out? Join us on another one of our wild adventures as we head out in search of the infamous wulfenite.

Table of Contents

Intro to Wulfenite

Characterized by its square tabular crystals, orange to yellow color, high luster and association with other lead minerals, wulfenite is found in the oxidized zones of hydrothermal lead deposits. Discovered in 1845, it is named after the Austrian Jesuit mineralogist, Franz Xavier von Wulfen (1728-1805).

A secondary mineral typically found as thin tabular crystals with a bright orange-red, yellow-orange, yellow or yellowish grey color in the oxidized zones of hydrothermal lead deposits.

In unique situations, it may precipitate from volcanic fumarole gas, in temperatures from 400 to 550°C. The mineral that is formed by super-heated mineral rich water being forced up from deep within the earth and into the cracks in the bedrock.

The minerals collect on each other as the water slowly cools and recedes leaving the cracks and pockets lined with fluorite and wulfenite crystals.

Although aesthetically magnificent wulfenite crystals are often too thin, soft, and sensitive to cut for jewelry, rare faceted pieces are greatly prized by collectors. The red of wulfenite, especially from the Red Cloud Mine in Arizona, is one of the richest colors in nature.

Many localities across the globe produce wulfenite's. However, cuttable material is very rare, indeed. Individual crystals usually have a tabular structure. As a result, they're frequently too thin to find a fragment suitable for cutting. Should a faceter acquire a suitable piece, even more challenges await.

These beautiful gems combine very low hardness with sensitivities to both heat and vibration. Although not well suited for jewelry use, faceted pieces, as well as crystals, make stunning collector's gems.

Red wulfenite over 1 carat and yellowish or orange stones over 2 carats are extremely scarce. The only larger stones come from Namibian (Tsumeb) material. However, this locality produced very few facetable gems very infrequently. Faceters have cut very few stones from this source.

<u>Wulfenite Fun Facts</u>

Under physical pressure, some wulfenite crystals may generate an electric charge. This is known as the piezoelectric effect. Piezoelectricity describes the ability of a mineral to develop electrical charges when put under stress. Piezoelectric minerals will develop charges when rubbed or struck repeatedly.

In modern times, piezoelectricity was named in the early 1800's when it was discovered that cane sugar, certain types of salt crystals, tourmaline, quartz, and topaz became electrified under pressure.

Yellow fluorescence in long-wave ultraviolet light has been observed in Wulfenite from a few localities. Fluorescence is a phenomenon that causes a mineral to "glow" in the within the visible spectrum when exposed to ultraviolet light. Minerals that exhibit fluorescence are known as "fluorescent minerals". Fluorescent minerals contain particles in their structure known as activators, which respond to ultraviolet light by giving off a visible glow.

Wulfenite is an enigma in terms of its symmetry. There are conflicting results of various symmetry tests and this usually does not happen. It is either a symmetry of 4 or 4/m. The difference is the disputed existence of a mirror plane perpendicular to the four-fold axis. If the mirror exists, then the crystals should have a top that is a mirror image of its bottom.

Although most crystals don't show it clearly, the bottom pyramidal faces slant at a different angle from the top pyramidal faces. This symmetrical oddity only adds to wulfenite's interest among serious collectors.

The Adventure

Picked up my buddy Dave at 5 in the morning. We were going after wulfenite. Our destination was a secret location located in Arizona. Well, maybe the location was not so secret but rather famous. The way to sneak in was a secret though. A secret to which I had the answer too.

As we drove thru the darkness we talked of past trips and the treasures we had collected over the years. We also spoke of what we had planned to collect in the future and before we knew it the sun had come up. We were on the dirt road making the 14-mile trip to the mine site.

The hills and valleys were in full spring bloom and were blanketed with colors of purple, yellow and red cactus flowers. Underneath the cactus flowers was a carpet of blue wild flowers. When we turned a corner, there was a small herd of big horn sheep grazing on the hillside just a few hundred feet off the road.

Soon after that we had reached our destination. The mine is enormous and it runs right next to a dirt road that cuts thru the hills and goes on for 20 miles to some sort of civilization. There is an access road that runs up to the main mining area that looks like something you would see in an old western movie.

Small shacks and bunk houses with broken windows and bullet holes and an old water tower. Where is John Wayne? Normally he would be facing down some bandits right here on this road, except he can't, because its blocked by a metal cable. There were several no trespassing signs hung across the cable, one of which read "Even if you know us don't cross his line". Woah not partner, these folks are serious!

This is truly an obstacle in the way of our day. Now I was taught that an obstacle is nothing more than a stepping stone to success and I used back country logic to get around this problem. We found a back-way in.

We drove down the main road about a mile and turned off on another small road and drove until we were out of sight. We stashed the truck and hiked in from the back side of the mine. We did not see or cross any no trespassing signs and according to my logic if we didn't see any signs and there were no signs how could we be trespassing?

The place was abandoned anyway, if we stayed out of sight no one would ever know. We were on the back side of a huge mine dump (all the dirt that had come from a huge pit that they had dug with tractors was dumped in a huge pile and the miners felt that it wasn't worth looking thru.)

There was orange wulfenite everywhere. This place was RICH! After 30 minutes of holding perfect pieces up and saying, "Dave look at this one, Dave look at this one", I held one up and said, "Dave is that a truck?" From the top of the dump pile which was as big as several football fields, was a brown truck that was heading straight for us. The driver slammed on the breaks, stopping right next to us engulfing us in a cloud of dust.

Busted! Before the dust settled the mine owner was out the door swearing and asking us if we could read. I was terrified. He was saying things like sheriff and jail along with several other obscenities. Uh oh. We are going to jail. What am I going to tell my family?

I can imagine what my wife was going to say to me. I put my chin in my chest, looked straight at the ground and started apologizing and that we thought the mine was abandoned. I then proceeded in telling him that we had come from another direction and didn't see all those signs.

I was talking a mile a minute then Dave decided to chime in. He began explaining to the owner that we had driven out from San Diego and that he had a claim on a mine himself. He then told the owner that he understood how he must have felt and we would pick up our things and leave right away.

Just like that all the anger left the owners face. "San Diego, my son is a marine and he is stationed in San Diego", he replied. "Can you get me into a tourmaline mine?" Dave replied "get you in? I have a claim on one, you can come any time you want." Dave had failed to tell him that he had never found anything there.

The next thing you know we were talking about mines, different rock clubs and field trips. I think he began to realize that we were just a couple of harmless old collectors just like him. After an hour of jolly old chit chat he told us that he had to leave and that we were welcome to stay and finish out the day.

He also told us that that if we ever wanted to come back we were to call him first before we revisited. We exchanged phone numbers and off we went. Unbelievable, we went from jail house to pent house just like that. Thanks Dave, you saved our asses. All too soon the sun began to set. We carried out our buckets threw the main entrance and set them next to the road.

No need to hide now, we knew the owner. That old saying obstacles being stepping stones to success came to mind at that moment. Dave stayed with our gear while I took a short hike to my pathfinder that we hid on the side road. When it came into sight it was nearly dark and all I could see were the two faded lights.

Faded headlights. I had forgotten to turn my headlights off when we hid the pathfinder. STRANDED!!!! Stranded in the middle of nowhere. No, worse than the middle of nowhere, we were in the middle of the desert. In the middle of nowhere there is no cell phone service. In the middle of the desert there is also no water.

No phone, no water, great we are going to die. A few days later I discovered that we were less than a mile from the Colorado river. Wish I would have known that sooner. I could see the headlines now "2 men die of dehydration next to the Colorado river." That's Dave and I for ya sometimes we got a lot on the ball and sometimes not so much.

I walked back to where Dave was waiting and gave him the bad news. He took it rather well but I could tell he was not happy. We quickly went back to the vehicle and tried to start it by pushing it backwards down a small hill. Can you jump start an automatic by pushing it down a little hill and into a gully? We couldn't. Nothing like being more stranded that you already were.

We pushed it until it was on a reasonably flat spot then we went back to the mine to light a signal fire. Plenty of wood there. All we had to do was tear it off our new friend's buildings. After a few hours of sitting around a cozy camp fire and relaxing we saw head lights in the distance, someone was coming.

We were saved! We threw more wood on the fire and when the care came into sight we waved and yelled. He went right by. We were too far from the main road, about fifty yards up the access road. Next car that comes I am running down the road to the main road yelling and screaming. Ya, that will work.

A few hours later more headlights, off I ran. It was so dark you couldn't see the ground. There was no way I could run. I slowly made my way down the hill as fast as I could without killing myself. I got half way down when the car drove by. No luck. I began to think our signal fire looked more like a camp fire.

Time to put the fire down next to the main road. Dave was quite comfortable and let me know that if there was any moving to be done it was up to me. I made several trips dragging wood down the road and made a fire. Is everyone worried at home? I was becoming lost in my thoughts. I should have been home a few hours ago. I was glad the owner was a nice guy.

We could have been sitting in jail rather than right here. Stranded but free. What if no one comes? Fifteen-mile hike to the ranger station, great. At about 1 am my wood was burned up and no more cars had come by so I decided to call it a night. Anyone driving in the middle of nowhere on a dirt road was probably not the rescuing type anyway. I was more likely to get robbed or worse.

Dave and I walked back to the pathfinder. I let the back seat down and there was enough room for the wo of us to lay cheek to cheek. Good thing I had an old beach towel to use as a blanket. It was mid-February and about 40 degrees. The towel made about a 2-degree difference. Just great. Good night Dave. Lights out.

I lay there thinking man this floor is so hard and uneven. It hurt and I had no way to get comfortable. It was impossible to get to sleep. What? What was that noise? Its Dave snoring. How could he fall asleep and so fast? Unbelievable. I lay there miserable all night and he just sawed logs, amazing. I watched the sun rise and what a sight. Framed by the rugged hills I had to admit it was beautiful.

I decided it was time to wake Dave up, we packed our backpacks for the long hike out of there. We talked of the possibilities of someone driving by and giving us a jump. We went back over o the mine to look for copper wire to use for jumper cable just in case. About ¾ of the way up the mine entrance road, parked about twenty feet off the side sat a small tractor.

I had spent half the night walking past it, too dark to see it. Tractors have batteries and this one had what looked like a new battery. All we had to do was take it out, carry it to the car and give it a try. More bad news. It was bolted in and we had no tools. We started looking around for something we could use to loosen the bolts.

I found a piece of metal with a hole in it that looked like it could work. After a little bit of pounding with a rock hammer we had a primitive wrench that did not work at all. An hour went by and very little progress had been made. Dave wanted to give up and he started walking before it got too hot.

I wasn't ready to give up. I knew our best chance was this battery and a half an hour later using a rock chisel, a hammer and my home-made wrench I had it out. Now to carry it to the car more than a half a mile away. It was twice the size of a regular truck battery and very heavy.

I could only go about fifty feet or so before I had to set it down to rest. I did that all the way to my car with no help from Dave. He was still a little pissed off at me. He will feel a lot better if this battery works. We had mine out and that one in within minutes.

I jumped in and inserted the key and turned. Boy what a sweet sound. My pathfinder fired right up. We loaded up and drove over to the tractor and took the batter out with the car still running. I didn't know you could do that but Dave did. We put it back into the tractor minus the hold down bolts, put my battery back in and drove home.

About the Cover Photo

When I found this piece, I was on the south-east side of the giant dump site. No one ever goes to that side and as a result it is less picked over. I was looking for tailings that were a little darker brown than the surrounding rocks and breaking them with my 2 lb hammer.

Every now and then you will come across one that has a small pocket with wulfenite crystals and the rock breaks right on the packet exposing these beautiful crystals to sunlight for the first time. That's just what happened I hit a rock about as big as my head it broke open and this beautiful little pocket was exposed.

ABOUT THE AUTHOR

As a little boy Jim Mellos got the rock bug from his uncle, who was a member of the Convair Gem and Mineral Club. He has fond memories of going through boxes of rocks that he had stored under his house, mostly from the same locations that Jim visits today. Jim joined the club and a year later became Field Trip Coordinator. Jim credits several members who had more experience in the field collecting with extending is knowledge.

Jim studied Marine Biology and Business Administration as UCSB and USD and was a pitcher on the baseball team for both schools. Currently, Jim is semi-retired and owns a business in Yuma, Arizona.

<u>Other Books By Jim Mellos</u>

Mining Natures Treasures with Jim and Dave: The Pocket paperback and eBook edition

https://www.amazon.com/Mining-Natures-Treasures-Jim-Dave/dp/1546909559

https://www.amazon.com/dp/B072JK8Y43

CONCLUSION

If you enjoyed this book, found it useful or otherwise then I'd really appreciate it if you would post a short review on Amazon. I do read all the reviews personally so that I can continually write what people are wanting.

Thanks for your support!

www.ingramcontent.com/pod-product-compliance
Lightning Source LLC
Chambersburg PA
CBHW050924290526
45792CB00002B/878